LEWIS & CLARK

TO THE PACIFIC

JOHN HAMILTON

VISIT US AT
WWW.ABDOPUB.COM

Published by ABDO & Daughters, an imprint of ABDO Publishing Company, 4940 Viking Drive, Suite 622, Edina, Minnesota 55435. Copyright ©2003 by Abdo Consulting Group, Inc. International copyrights reserved in all countries. No part of this book may be reproduced in any form without written permission from the publisher.

Printed in the United States.

Edited by Paul Joseph
Graphic Design: John Hamilton
Cover Design: Mighty Media
Photos and illustrations:
    John Hamilton, Cover, p. 1, 4, 7, 8, 10, 14, 17-30
    American Philosophical Society, p. 12, 13, 16, 21, 24
    John F. Clymer, Clymer Museum of Art, p. 11, 29
    Library of Congress, W. Clark, p. 3, 30-31
    Library of Congress, E.S. Curtis, p. 5, 6, 9, 12, 28
    Oregon Historical Society, p. 15

Library of Congress Cataloging-in-Publication Data

Hamilton, John, 1959-
    To the Pacific / John Hamilton.
    p. cm.—(Lewis & Clark)
    Includes bibliographical references and index.
    Summary: Joins the Lewis and Clark Expedition in the fall of 1805 near Weippe, Idaho, as they travel to Gray's Bay, twenty miles from the Pacific Ocean, and build Fort Clatsop as a winter home. Includes highlights and directions to historical points of interest.
    ISBN 1-57765-765-9
    1. Lewis and Clark Expedition (1804-1806)—Juvenile literature. 2. West (U.S.)—Discovery and exploration—Juvenile literature. 3. West (U.S.)—Description and travel—Juvenile literature. 4. Overland journeys to the Pacific—Juvenile literature. [1. Lewis and Clark Expedition (1804-1806) 2. West (U.S.)—Discovery and exploration. 3. Overland journeys to the Pacific.] I. Title.

F592.7.H275 2002
917.804'2—dc21

2001053397

TABLE OF CONTENTS

The Real People 5

Downstream 10

Waterfalls 15

To the Ocean 19

Cape Disappointment 23

Fort Clatsop 27

If You Go Today 30

Glossary 31

Web Sites 31

Index 32

"The pleasure I now felt in having triumphed over the rocky Mountains…can be more readily conceived than expressed."
MERIWETHER LEWIS

THE REAL PEOPLE

*I*n the autumn of 1805, Meriwether Lewis led the Corps of Discovery out of the Bitterroot Mountains. After 11 grueling days, covering 160 miles (257 km), with little or nothing to eat, they emerged from the wilderness weak and vulnerable—right in the middle of the most powerful Native American tribe in the Pacific Northwest.

Several days earlier, Captain William Clark and six other men had gone ahead in a desperate attempt to find food. They found a horse, which they killed and butchered. Along with the horsemeat, Clark left a note for Captain Lewis, telling him that he intended to push onward as quickly as possible. He hoped to make it off the mountains and onto the plains, where game was more plentiful.

When the main expedition found the horse Clark had left for them, Captain Lewis was optimistic that their ordeal through the mountains was nearing an end. Finding the horse

meant that Native Americans were nearby. In his journal, Lewis wrote that they "made a hearty meal on our horse beef much to the comfort of our hungry stomachs."

Left: Black Eagle, a Nez Percé warrior, was photographed by Edward S. Curtis a century after the Lewis and Clark expedtion.
Far left: A grove of cedar trees growing along the Lolo Trail in the Bitterroot Mountains, in present-day Idaho.

On September 22, 1805, they emerged from the mountains. Somehow, they had avoided freezing to death, or falling to their doom over the narrow mountain pathway. They were half starved, but they were in open country now. By the end of the day, they came to an Indian village of 18 lodges near present-day Weippe, Idaho. The Native Americans welcomed the Corps of Discovery. The Indians called themselves Nimiipu—"the real people."

Captain Clark, who arrived at the village days earlier, had already started taking notes on the tribe's sophisticated, complex society. They were skilled warriors, but they also prized family relationships. The elderly were honored most of all.

This Nez Percé warrior chief was photographed by Edward S. Curtis.

Through the sign language of one of the French-Canadian interpreters, Clark made a faulty translation of their name, calling them "pierced nose," or Nez Percé, even though nose piercing wasn't a common practice among the tribe.

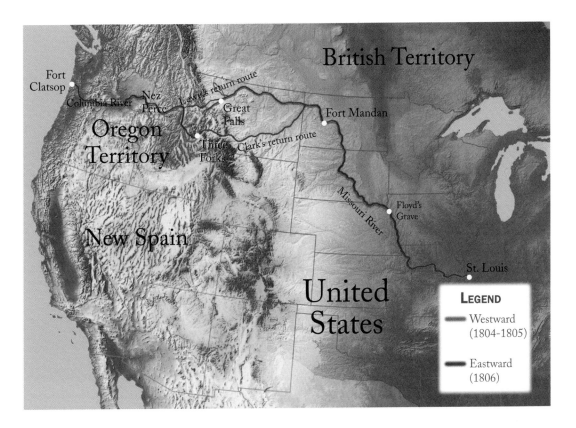

Clark befriended one of the chiefs, an older man called Twisted Hair. On a white elkskin, Twisted Hair drew a map of the area west of the villages. Clark learned that the nearby Clearwater River joined with the Snake River, which in turn emptied into the Columbia River. The Corps's days of trekking overland were over. Soon they would be back on the water, paddling downstream this time, speeding toward the Pacific Ocean.

Clark joined Lewis and the main party on the night of September 22. Clark wrote in his journal, "I found Capt Lewis & the party Encamped, much fatigued, & hungery, much rejoiced to find something to eate of which They appeared to partake plentifully."

Through his own bad experience, Clark warned them not to overeat the dried salmon and camas roots given by the Nez Percé. In his journal entry two days earlier, he had written, "I find myself verry unwell all the evening from eateing the fish & roots too freely." The next day he wrote, "I am verry Sick today and puke…"

The Clearwater River, which Lewis and Clark paddled down toward the Columbia River

The men didn't heed Clark's warning—they were starving and needed to eat. They gorged themselves on the food the Nez Percé provided. Soon they too became violently ill, suffering severe diarrhea and vomiting. They had lived on a diet of meat for so long that the switch to fish and roots caused terrible indigestion. There may also have been bacteria on the fish, but since the Indians didn't also get sick, the illness was probably caused by the change of diet.

To make matters worse, Clark gave the men several doses of Rush's Thunderbolts, medicine they had brought with them from the East. Lewis and Clark believed the pills could cure almost any illness with their powerful laxative effect. It was the worst thing they could have done. The diarrhea got more severe, likely causing dehydration, which only made them sicker.

Over the next two weeks, the journal entries resembled the logbook of a hospital emergency room. Lewis was especially ill. Clark wrote, "Capt. Lewis scercely able to ride on a jentle horse… Several men So unwell that they were Compelled to lie on the Side of the [trail]…"

While the Corps was incapacitated by illness, the Nez Percé met secretly to decide what to do with these weak strangers who were so wealthy with weapons and tools. The men of the expedition were the first white people the Nez Percé had ever encountered. There was serious talk about killing them and taking their possessions, which would be an easy enough task. The Corps's modern rifles would make the Nez Percé extremely powerful.

An old woman stepped forward, begging her people to spare the strangers' lives. Her name was Watkuweis, which meant "Returned from a Faraway Country." As a young girl, she had been kidnapped by Blackfeet Indians, then sold into slavery. While in Canada, she was befriended by white people. She finally escaped and somehow found her way back to the Nez Percé villages.

A Nez Percé named Many Moons told how Watkuweis shared her story with the tribe: "She told history about the whites and every Nez Percé listened… told how the white people were good to her, treated her with kindness. That is why the Nez Percé never made harm to the Lewis and Clark people… We ought to have a monument to her in this far West. She saved much for the white race."

Raven Blanket, a Nez Percé chief, was photographed by Edward S. Curtis

Once again, an Indian woman saved the Corps. First an old Shoshone woman, then Sacagawea, and now Watkuweis. Lewis and Clark owed much of their success to Native Americans, which they barely acknowledged in their journals. Seventy two years later, in 1877, the U.S. Army drove Chief Joseph and the Nez Percé from Idaho. Among Chief Joseph's people were old men and women who were children when Lewis and Clark passed through, and who remembered the kindness and restraint Twisted Hair's people had shown the Corps of Discovery.

DOWNSTREAM

Rapids of the Clearwater River

For nearly two weeks the Corps of Discovery worked at building five dugout canoes, in between bouts of diarrhea and vomiting. They worked in a grove of ponderosa pine trees along the Clearwater River. They called the place Canoe Camp. They chopped down several trees, but they were too weak to use their tools to hollow out the boats. Chief Twisted Hair showed them an easier Indian method that used a slow-burning fire trench to burn out the logs.

The men were feeling better from their sickness, but the recovery process was slow:

Oct. 4: "Capt Lewis & my Self eate a Supper of roots boiled, which filled us So full of wind, that we were Scercely able to Breathe all night…"

WILLIAM CLARK

Twisted Hair promised to care for the Corps' ponies until they returned the next spring. Lewis had each horse branded with the mark "U.S., Capt. M. Lewis." Twisted Hair also agreed to go partway downstream with the Corps, guiding them and informing other Native Americans that the Corps came in peace. Another chief, Tetoharsky, also joined them.

On October 7, they pushed their five dugout canoes into the Clearwater River. Finally, they had a swift current behind them. Spirits soared, even though many of the men were still weak and sick. Twisted Hair told them it would be a journey of only a couple of weeks until they reached the ocean.

The expedition raced down the Clearwater, then linked with the Snake River. They encountered many strong rapids along the way. Still, they preferred running the rapids to the time-consuming process of portaging their canoes and baggage. The season was getting on, and Lewis and Clark knew they had to set up a fort on the coast before winter set in. Also, a growing sense of triumph infected the men. They were very close to their goal of crossing the continent. They were in a hurry; the rapids slowed them down, but they still managed to travel up to 30 miles (48 km) a day.

Gradually the men recovered, gaining strength day by day. They grew more daring in shooting the roaring whitewater, despite the cumbersome design of the dugout canoes. It was dangerous work: the canoes were tossed about and swamped, or crashed on rocks and sprang leaks. Old Toby, the Shoshone Indian who had safely guided the Corps over the Bitterroot Mountains, was so scared of the rapids that one morning he took off for home, leaving without pay.

John Clymer's *Angry River* shows the Corps shooting the rapids of the Columbia River system

A sketch of a white salmon trout from the Lewis and Clark journals

Native Americans were everywhere. They gathered on the riverbanks and watched as the canoes passed by. They arrived in camp to trade, swap stories, or be entertained by Pierre Cruzatte's fiddle playing and the men's dancing.

When they were on the Great Plains, the expedition often went hundreds of miles in between Indian settlements. Here, they saw Native Americans almost every day. Nez Percé, Wananpum, Yakima, and Walla Walla Indians turned out by the hundreds to see the strangers. Luckily, most were friendly. Twisted Hair and Tetoharsky went ahead and informed their relatives that the white men were coming. The presence of Sacagawea also helped. She was a sign to the Indians that the white people came in peace.

"The sight of this Indian woman, wife to one of our interprs. confirmed those people of our friendly intentions, as no woman ever accompanies a war party of Indians in this quarter."

WILLIAM CLARK

A Wishram fisherman nets salmon in the Columbia River

Soon the expedition made it to the Columbia River. They were astonished at the millions of salmon swimming in the crystal-clear waters. The Walla Walla tribe, which lived on the banks of the Columbia, depended on salmon and had plenty to trade. But the men of the Corps didn't want to risk getting sick again. They traded with the Walla Wallas for dozens of dogs, which everyone ate with great relish. Everyone, that is, except William Clark. "Our diet extremely bad," he wrote.

They were moving through a semi-desert now. Game was scarce and so was firewood. Instead of sending out teams of hunters, they saved time by purchasing dogs from the Indians. Lewis said the diet of dog meat kept the men healthy, but Clark hated it. "As for my own part," he wrote in his journal, "I have not become reconsiled to the taste of this animal."

A page from the journals of Lewis and Clark show the intersection of the Snake, Columbia, and Yakima Rivers

"We passed safe, to the astonishment of all the Indians."

WILLIAM CLARK

WATERFALLS

On October 18, 1805, Captain Clark climbed a tall cliff and saw, off in the distance, a snow-covered mountain he thought was Mount St. Helens. Even though it was actually Mount Adams, Clark had spied the Cascade Range, which had been seen 13 years earlier by British explorers coming up the Columbia from the Pacific. Lewis and Clark were back on the map. They had crossed a continent and connected east with west.

On October 23, they entered a 55-mile (89-km) stretch of the river with narrow channels surrounded by towering cliffs. The Columbia River Gorge contained a series of spectacular and dangerous waterfalls and rapids. The first was Celilo Falls. They were forced to portage around most of it. They followed their canoes down part of it with sections of rope made from elkskin. Local Indians helped carry the baggage around the falls.

The Indians in the area were Chinooks, enemies of the Nez Percé. At a place called The Dalles, Twisted Hair and Tetoharsky said good-bye to Lewis and Clark and began the long journey home.

Below: Celilo Falls no longer exists today. It was submerged when a hydroelectric dam was built in 1957.
Far left: A waterfall tumbles toward the mighty Columbia River Gorge.

At a raging waterfall called the Short Narrows of The Dalles, Clark and Cruzatte, the Corps's best boatman, went to a high cliff to scout the river. The Chinook Indians said the raging whitewater was impassible. Clark and Cruzatte thought otherwise, even though Clark was aghast at "the horrid appearance of this agitated gut Swelling, boiling & whorling in every direction."

Clark had the men portage the most important cargo around the falls, including the journals, the rifles and ammunition, plus the scientific instruments. Today, the Short Narrows would be classified a Class V rapid, too dangerous to run even with the best equipment. Clark and Cruzatte pushed off into the swirling current in a cumbersome dugout canoe.

Hundreds of Indians watched from the cliffs above, waiting to see the crazy white men kill themselves in the furious current. They were also eager to help themselves to any cargo that might wash up after the strangers had drowned. But Clark and Cruzatte shot straight through. "We passed safe," Clark wrote, "to the astonishment of all the Indians." Clark was pleased with himself, although, he wrote, "from the top of the rock [the water] did not appear as bad as when I was in it."

A sketch of the Long and Short Narrows of the Columbia River, from the journals of Lewis and Clark

Lewis & Clark

The Corps ran other "impassable" rapids through the Columbia River Gorge, although sometimes they were forced to portage. Finally, on November 2, they made it past the final waterfall. On November 3, they passed and named Beacon Rock. At this point they began noticing the Columbia River rising and falling with the tide. The ocean couldn't be far away.

Beacon Rock, in present-day Washington, along the north shore of the Columbia River

"Ocian in view. O! the joy."

WILLIAM CLARK

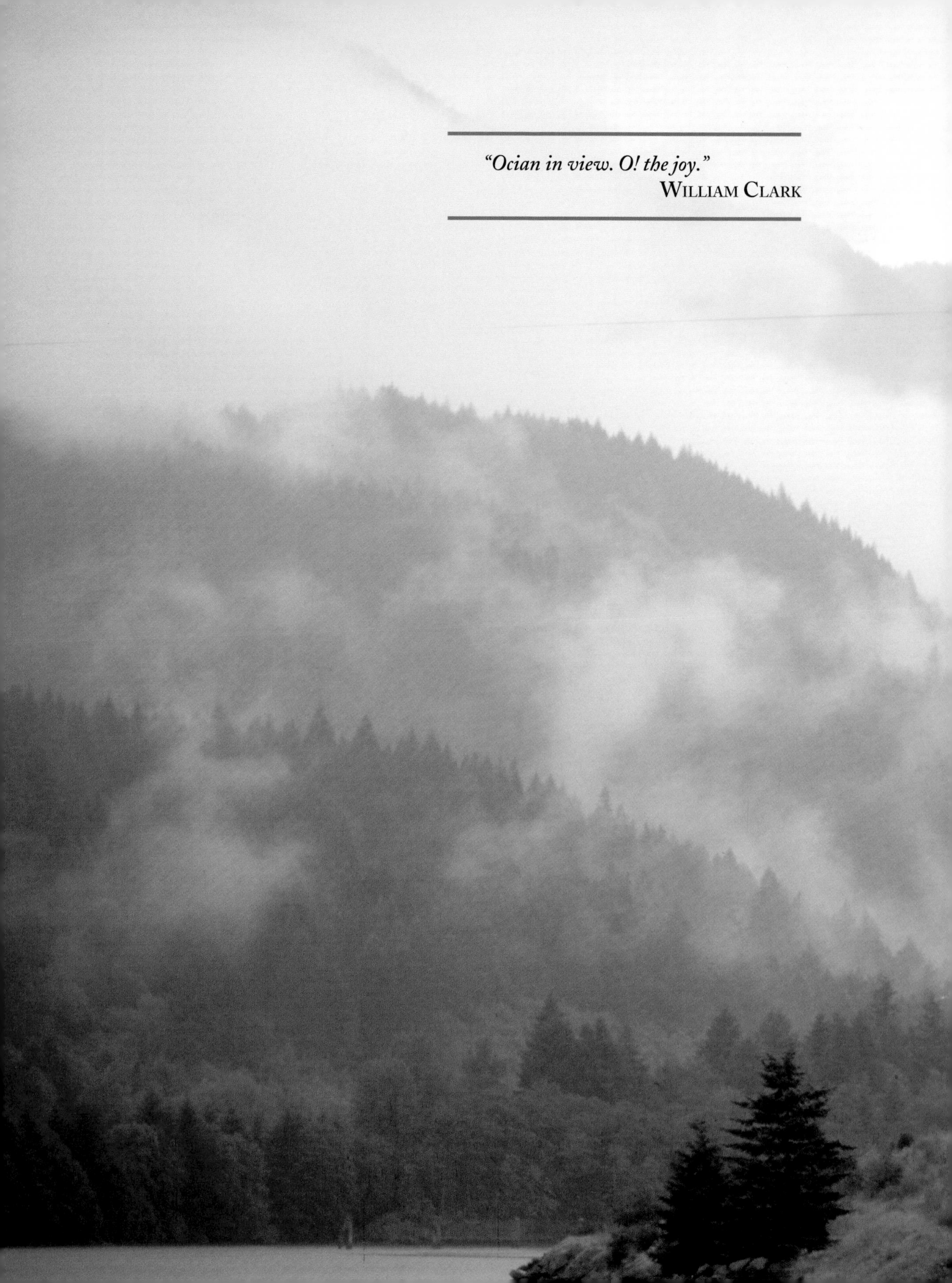

TO THE OCEAN

After passing through the raging falls of the Columbia River Gorge, the expedition entered a new climate zone. It was wet most of the time, because the winds from the ocean stalled against the Cascade Range and produced a steady drizzle. Lush forests filled with fir, ash, and spruce enveloped both shores. The trees were huge, the biggest the men had ever seen. Waterfalls poured down from the surrounding cliffs. Dense fog blanketed the river valley. Sometimes the morning fog was so thick they had to wait for hours before setting out.

The river hosted a multitude of geese, swans, ducks, and brants. A happy William Clark was finally able to eat roast duck, setting aside the dog meat that caused him so much distress.

The expedition passed many Chinook Indian villages. The Native Americans often visited the Corps when they were camped for the night. Lewis and Clark thought the Chinooks were highly skilled at making canoes and navigating them in rough water. But for the most part the captains didn't much like the Chinooks. There were several reasons for this, including a language barrier. The Corps had no interpreters that spoke Chinookan, and the Chinooks didn't use sign language like the Nez Percé or the Plains Indian tribes. Lewis and Clark used Chinook jargon, which was a very basic language combining Chinook, English, French, and Nootka. Translations were often garbled, and misunderstandings caused bad feelings.

The Columbia River widened as the Corps paddled closer to the ocean

The Chinook tribes were used to trading with Europeans who passed by the mouth of the Columbia River. These Europeans often dealt in the sea otter trade. The Chinooks learned to drive a hard bargain, and the captains grew to resent the high prices they were forced to pay for food.

More seriously, some of the Chinooks engaged in petty theft when visiting camp. As the expedition's supply of trade goods dwindled, the captains grew angrier.

Adding to their discomfort was the constant rain. Everything became waterlogged. "We are all wet cold and disagreeable," wrote Clark in his journal. Still they paddled downstream, the river widening as they went.

Finally, on the afternoon of November 7, a fog lifted off the river, revealing a most welcome sight. The men shouted as William Clark reached for his notebook and jotted down his now-famous words: "Ocian in view! O! the joy."

That night in camp, he wrote in his journal, "Great joy in camp we are in view of the Ocian, this great Pacific Octean which we have been So long anxious to See. And the roreing or

noise made by the waves braking on the rockey Shores may be heard distinctly."

Clark calculated the distance they had traveled since leaving St. Louis and came up with a staggering 4,142 miles (6,666 km). His estimate would later be proven accurate to within 40 miles (64 km), a remarkable feat of dead reckoning.

Dense, moss-laden forests line the Columbia River Estuary

William Clark's famous journal entry of November 7, 1805: "Ocian in view! O! the joy."

"The emence Seas and waves…roars like an emence fall at a distance, and this roaring has continued ever Since our arrival…"

WILLIAM CLARK

Cape Disappointment

What Clark thought was the Pacific was actually an estuary of the ocean, at the eastern end of Gray's Bay. The ocean was still 20 miles (32 km) away. As the expedition paddled toward the mouth of the Columbia River, fierce winter weather settled in, sending high waves crashing down on their dugout canoes. They were forced to retreat to shore.

For nearly three weeks they were pinned down on the north side of the river. With high cliffs at their backs and raging water in front of them, they were often trapped. They made a series of stops, clawing their way downstream and camping in small, virtually unprotected coves as giant waves lashed against the shore. Thunder, lightning, and high winds added to the misery. Huge driftwood logs, many feet thick and some more than 200 feet (61 m) long, crashed into camp as the swells surged upward. Clark wrote that it was "the most disagreeable time I have experienced."

On November 15 they camped on a sandy beach. The waves were too high for them to pass any farther. It was the end of the trail west for the expedition.

Below: A storm lashes Oregon's Cannon Beach, south of the mouth of the Columbia River *Far left:* Flowers growing on a cliff overlooking the Pacific Ocean

Beach grasses flutter in the wind near present-day Seaside, Oregon

They set up camp, and then for several days Lewis and Clark did some exploring on the north side of the shore. Most of the men stayed in camp, warmed by their fires and marveling at their accomplishment. "Men appear much Satisfied with their trip," wrote Clark, "beholding with estonishment the high waves dashing against the rocks & this emence ocian."

The small expeditions exploring the north shore were looking for food, and for European trading vessels. If they were lucky, they could flag one down and trade for supplies, or even a ride back to the east. But they had no such luck.

"Our officers named this Cape, Cape disappointment, on account of not finding Vessells there."

JOSEPH WHITEHOUSE

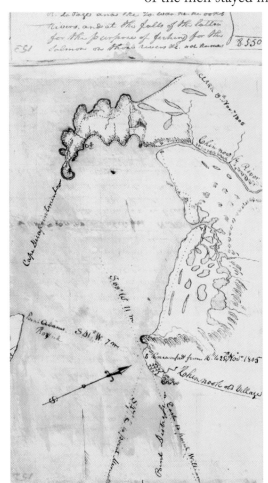

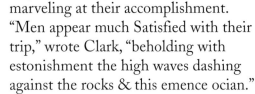

William Clark's map shows the mouth of the Columbia River. Although Joseph Whitehouse thought Lewis and Clark named Cape Disappointment, it actually got its name years earlier by a seafaring explorer who had trouble navigating into the river.

On November 24, everyone was called together. A decision had to be made: where would they spend the winter? They could stay on the north side of the Columbia, but there wasn't much game, and the Chinook Indians were charging high prices for food. They could paddle across the estuary to the south side, in present-day Oregon, where there were more elk and where the Clatsop Indians seemed more willing to trade at reasonable prices. Or they could move back upstream where it was drier, perhaps to the Nez Percé villages.

The captains called for a vote. It was an extraordinary moment. They could have decided themselves and then forced the Corps to obey; it was a military expedition, after all. But they had grown to be a family, a group of people who worked as a team, and every team-member's voice counted. York, Clark's slave, was allowed to vote almost 60 years before slaves were freed in the United States. Sacagawea also voted, more than 100 years before women or Indians became full citizens.

Sea gulls scavenge for food along a beach in Oregon. In the background is Tillamook Head.

"At this place we...wintered and remained from the 7th Decr. 1805 to this day and have lived as well as we had a right to expect..."

WILLIAM CLARK

FORT CLATSOP

*T*he majority of the party voted to cross the Columbia and spend the winter on the south side of the river. It would still be wet and stormy, but there was more elk to hunt. Plus, there was a chance they might spot a passing ship and hitch a ride home. And even if a ship never came, there was no rush to press eastward: they had to wait until July at the earliest for the snows to melt before they could cross the Bitterroot Mountains.

After a treacherous crossing of the storm-tossed estuary, the Corps set up camp a few miles from the coast. They found a good freshwater supply in a spruce forest on a river near present-day Astoria, Oregon. There they built Fort Clatsop, which they named after the friendly Clatsop Indian tribe.

By Christmas of 1805, they had moved into their new fort. It was a log stockade 50 feet (15 m) square. Two rows of cabins were separated by a small parade ground. On one side were the enlisted men's quarters, plus storage rooms. On the other side were the captains' quarters, a meat storage room, and a room for Toussaint Charbonneau, Sacagawea, and their infant son, Jean Baptiste.

During the winter, Lewis and Clark worked on their maps and journals, generally noting everything that had happened to them on the journey so far.

Right: An actor at Fort Clatsop National Memorial demonstrates how the men fired their rifles.
Left: The reconstructed Fort Clatsop was built near the original site in 1955, southwest of Astoria, Oregon.

In January 1806, a whale washed ashore on Cannon Beach, south of the Corps's salt-making camp. They bought 300 pounds (136 kg) of blubber from the Tillamook Indians to supplement their meager diet at Fort Clatsop.

"January 17th. Continued stormey all last night, and this morning Wet & rainey."

JOSEPH WHITEHOUSE

The men, meanwhile, kept busy hunting elk and deer, making candles and moccasins, sewing clothes, and boiling sea water to make salt. They were preparing for the long journey home in the spring, and they were anxious to get going. The men were homesick, and the dreary weather didn't help. It rained on all but 12 days during their stay at Fort Clatsop. The food was bad: in the wet weather, meat spoiled very quickly. To make matters worse, the men were infested with fleas, which, Clark wrote, "torment us in such a manner as to deprive us of half the nights Sleep."

Ferns and moss grow on the damp roof of Lewis and Clark's quarters at Fort Clatsop. For most of their stay at the fort, the weather was "rainy, wet, and disagreeable."

There were frequent visits by Clatsop and Chinook Indians, but the Corps was quickly running out of gifts to use as trade barter. Everything was in short supply, and they still had half a continent to cross. They would be heading home this time, however, and once they crossed the Bitterroot Mountains, the Missouri River would propel them downstream all the way to St. Louis.

But before they reached civilization, before they could be reunited with their families, they first had to wait out the winter in the dreary, boring, wet confines of Fort Clatsop.

Then they could go home.

Above: John Clymer's *Sacagawea at the Big Water*
Below left: A reproduction of the salt camp the Corps ran near present-day Seaside, Oregon, about 10 miles (16 km) from Fort Clatsop. Seawater was boiled in five buckets placed on top of fire-heated rocks. After the water evaporated, salt was scraped off the insides of the buckets.

IF YOU GO TODAY

FORT CLATSOP NATIONAL MEMORIAL

Built in 1955, this reconstruction of Fort Clatsop sits near the original site of the Corps of Discovery's 1805-1806 winter quarters. Run today by the National Park Service, Fort Clatsop is based on a floor plan drawn by William Clark on the elkhide cover of his fieldbook. Living history demonstrations by the park's staff in period costume show many of the frontier skills used by Lewis and Clark. In addition to touring the fort, you can also hike on trails leading to the expedition's canoe landing and the spring where the Corps drew their fresh water.

ECOLA STATE PARK, CANNON BEACH, OR

Cannon Beach is where the Corps found the remains of a whale that had washed up on shore. Today, this is a day-use park where you can see bird rookeries, sea lions, and herds of elk. There is also a scenic cliff hiking trail over Tillamook Head.

COLUMBIA RIVER GORGE NATIONAL SCENIC AREA

The Columbia River Gorge is a river canyon that cuts a water route through the Cascade Range. There are more than 50 miles (80 km) of attractions on both the Washington and Oregon sides of the gorge, including spectacular waterfalls, state parks, campsites, wildflowers, hiking trails, water sports, and many other outdoor activities. At Bonneville Dam, you can take a tour of the dam that inundated the cascades of the Columbia River. There is also a fish hatchery, trails, and a Lewis and Clark exhibit.

GLOSSARY

CORPS

A branch of the military that has a specialized function.

DEAD RECKONING

A way of estimating distance based on data in a written logbook, such as speed and time spent going in a certain direction. For example, when traveling upriver, one might estimate that a certain bend in the river is a mile away. Once you get to the bend, you estimate the distance to the next bend, or other landmark, like a big tree or island. At the end of the day, you add up all the figures to get the total distance traveled on the river. Some people are very skilled at dead reckoning. William Clark estimated that near the mouth of the Columbia River the Corps had traveled 4,142 miles (6,666 km) from St. Louis. Scientists using more precise methods later showed that Clark was only 40 miles (64 km) off!

GREAT PLAINS

A huge, sloping region of valleys and plains in west-central North America. The Great Plains extend from Texas to southern Canada, and from the Rocky Mountains nearly 400 miles (644 km) to the east.

PORTAGE

To carry a boat and supplies overland from one lake or river to another. The Corps of Discovery portaged around the Great Falls of Montana for more than 18 miles (29 km).

WEB SITES

Would you like to learn more about Lewis & Clark? Please visit **www.abdopub.com** to find up-to-date Web site links about Lewis & Clark and the Corps of Discovery. These links are routinely monitored and updated to provide the most current information available.

INDEX

A
Army, U.S. 9
Astoria, OR 27

B
Beacon Rock 17
Bitterroot Mountains 5, 11, 12, 27, 29
Blackfeet 9

C
Canada 9
Canoe Camp 10
Cape Disappointment 24
Cascade Mountains 15, 19
Celilo Falls 15
Charbonneau, Jean Baptiste 27
Charbonneau, Toussaint 27
Chief Joseph 9
Chinook 15, 16, 19, 20, 25, 29
Clark, William 5, 6, 7, 8, 9, 10, 11, 12, 14, 15, 16, 18, 19, 20, 21, 22, 23, 24, 25, 26, 27, 28

Clatsop 25, 27, 29
Clearwater River 7, 10, 11
Columbia River 7, 12, 15, 17, 19, 20, 23, 25, 27
Columbia River Gorge 15, 17, 19
Corps of Discovery 5, 6, 7, 9, 10, 11, 12, 16, 17, 19, 25, 27, 29
Cruzatte, Pierre 12, 16

D
Dalles, The 15, 16

F
Fort Clatsop 27, 28, 29

G
Gass, Patrick 10
Gray's Bay 23
Great Plains 12

I
Idaho 9

L
Lewis, Meriwether 4, 5, 7, 8, 9, 10, 11, 12, 15, 19, 24, 27

M
Many Moons 9
Missouri River 29
Mount Adams 15
Mount St. Helens 15

N
Nez Percé 6, 7, 8, 9, 12, 15, 19, 25
Nimiipu 6
Nootka 19

O
Old Toby 11
Oregon 25

P
Pacific Ocean 5, 7, 15, 20, 23
Plains Indians 19

R
Rocky Mountains 4
Rush's Thunderbolts 8

S
Sacagawea 9, 12, 25, 27
Short Narrows 16
Shoshone 9, 11
Snake River 7, 11
St. Louis 21, 29

T
Tetoharsky 10, 12, 15
Twisted Hair 7, 9, 10, 11, 12, 15

W
Walla Walla 12
Wananpum 12
Watkuweis 9
Weippe, ID 6
Whitehouse, Joseph 24, 28

Y
Yakima 12
York 25